AF255594

The Ride

Linda Rae Schaal

Cover and Interior Design: Rebecca Finkel, F + P Graphic Design, FPGD.com
Book Consultant: Judith Briles, TheBookShepherd.com

Published by Raelin Press
Books may be purchased in quantity by contacting the publisher
through the author's website: www.LindaRaeSchaal.com

Library of Congress Control Number: 2022923679
ISBN IS hardcover: 978-1-955705-12-7
ISBN KDP softcover: 978-1-955705-13-4
ISBN eBook: 978-1-955705-14-1
Inspirational | Spiritual | Poetry | Photography

First Edition

Dedicated to my late husband,

Ruben Schaal Jr. (RJ)

the father of my sons and love of my life.

A true inspiration to so many and a towering example

of an ordinary man who led an extraordinary life

in the midst of the battles he himself faced.

But those who wait on the Lord shall renew their strength;

they shall mount up with wings like eagles.

They shall run and not be weary.

They shall walk and not faint.

—Isaiah 40:31 (NKJV)

Author's Note

I truly love to write and am compelled to share my experience and perspective, from the most challenging of circumstances to the most exhilarating of successes. From personal observation and imagination to my inquisitions and resolutions, along with the obvious mishaps, blunders, quirks and frustrations.

In doing so, I am continually rediscovering myself and my potential while fueling my passion for believing that we are all uniquely created for such a time as this.

A poem, you ask? A rhyme, you muse? Almost too simple but, wait, read deeper. Let the words, the rhyme, the reality, carry you because we've all been there!

The Ride is a reflection of my journey through life, encompassing battles such as we all face. Join me now for **The Ride** … just you and me. May it encourage and inspire all who see, who touch, who feel...

Linda Rae

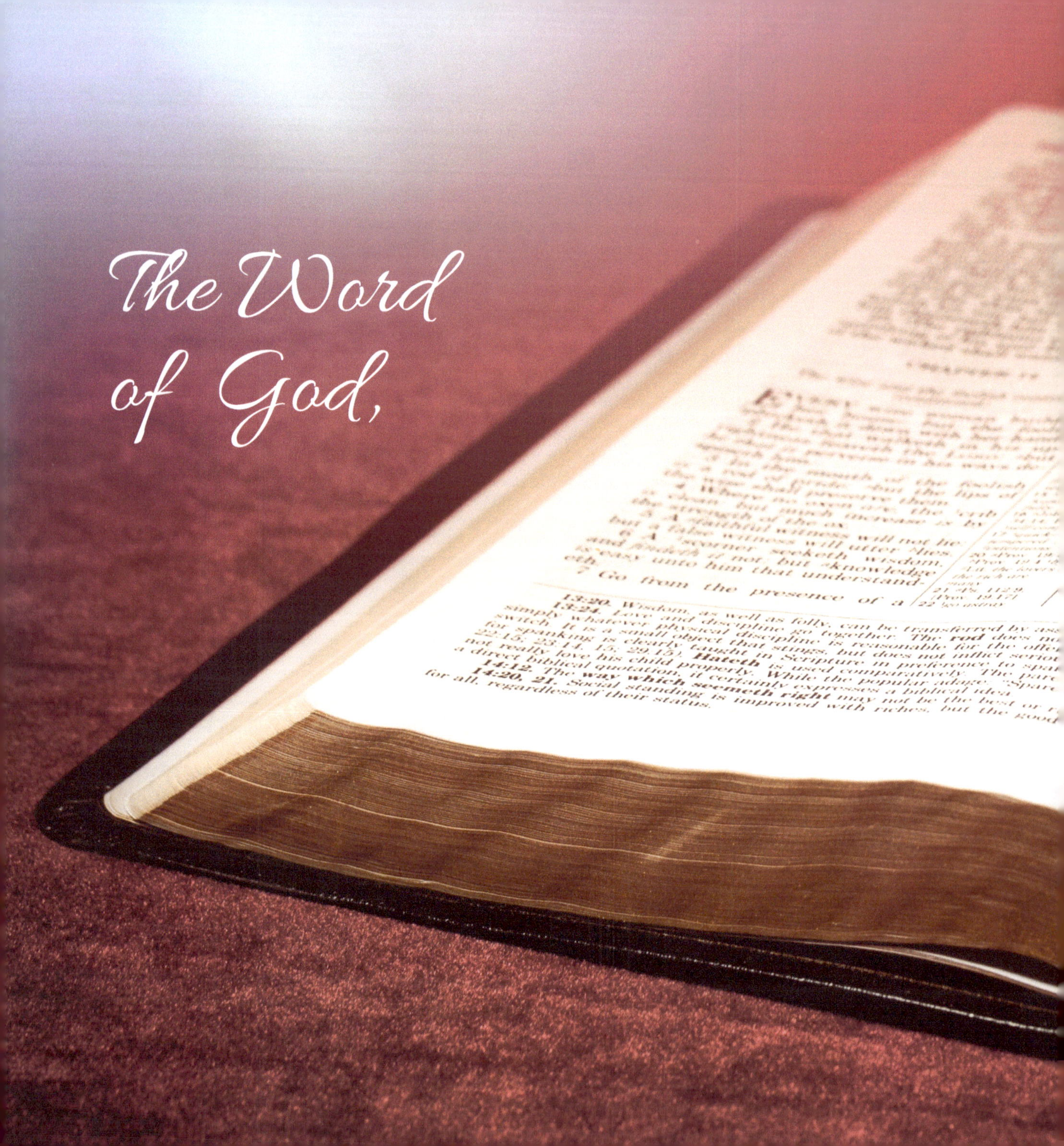
The Word
of God,

my strength,

my rod,

carries me to fight.

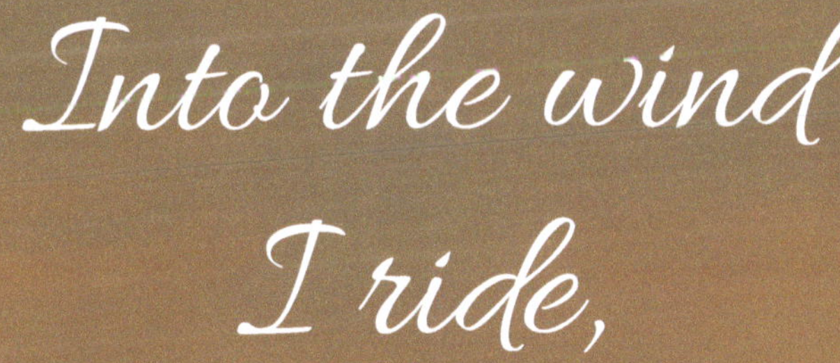
Into the wind
I ride,

and then

I charge

into the night!

The wretched course

that stretches forth

will crumble
under grace,

bestowed anew

to lead me through

this battle
I must face.

Bible

I trust indeed

the mighty steed

with whom

I now embark,

as one

who bares
my soul,

and dares

to race

into the dark.

For in my sight

there dawns

the light

that is to be

my guide.

And there

I see

my victory,

the prize

toward which
I ride...

The Ride

The Word of God,
my strength, my rod,
carries me to fight.
Into the wind I ride, and then
I charge into the night!

The wretched course that stretches forth
will crumble under grace,
bestowed anew to lead me through
this battle I must face.

I trust indeed the mighty steed
with whom I now embark,
as one who bares my soul, and dares
to race into the dark.

For in my sight there dawns the light
that is to be my guide.
And there I see my victory,
the prize toward which I ride...

The Lord your God

is with you wherever you go.

—from Joshua 1:9 (NKJV)

International bestselling author Linda Rae Schaal shares hundreds of her life observations of family, friends, and fans within **Seasonal Salt.** With her whirl of words that create a kaleidoscope of color, inspiration, and joy, readers will delight as each page turns.

A Pearl of A Different Kind

Oh, that the flower would not die;

Oh, that it would not cease;

for it is the embodiment

of purity and peace …

Oh, that its beauty could exist

beyond the span of time;

soft as that of a mother's kiss,

a pearl of a different kind.

You are the salt of the earth and the light of the world.
—from Matthew 5: 13-14

About the Author

Linda Rae Schaal is a Colorado author, born and raised in Southern California in the 1950's. An entrepreneur with over 50 years of experience in the business world, this mother of two and grandmother of eight, began publishing her work in local newspapers and regional magazines at the urging of her late husband. She draws her inspiration from life through her strong faith and personal experiences, coupled with a passion for bringing people together.

Linda examines the world around her and embraces living, with unique insight; acutely tuned to the emotional, often sensitive and surprisingly humorous everyday circumstances in which any one of us might find ourselves.

Linda has written over a thousand narratives, poems, musings and quotes, which are featured in *Seasonal Salt*. A delightful journey into the world of discovery with critters and friendship, *Clea the Clever Caterpillar* children's book series is at the heart of a young reader's imagination. *The Ride* is a personally inspired, richly poetic gift book combining vivid and powerful images with Linda's heartfelt prose.

www.LindaRaeSchaal.com